Front cover: Lo que queda del aire   1987
              What is left of the air
              pencil and ink   (109 x 150)cm

First published May 1988 by GMP Publishers Ltd
  P O Box 247, London N15 6RW, UK
Individual pictures world copyright © 1988 Roberto González Fernández
This collection world copyright © 1988 GMP Publishers Ltd

British Library Calaloguing in Publication Data

González Fernández, Roberto, *1948*-
  Journeys.
  I. Spanish visual arts. González Fernández,
  Roberto, 1948-
  I. Title
  709'.2'4

  ISBN 0-85449-070-1

Printed,bound and reproduced in Hongkong by South Sea International Press Ltd.

Roberto González Fernández

JOURNEYS

artworks

introduced by
John Russell Taylor
the artist in conversation with
Javier Mazorra

ROBERTO GONZÁLEZ FERNÁNDEZ

Most of the contemporary Hispanic artists we know best and see most — Botero, Claudio Bravo — are in fact Latin American. Roberto González Fernández is Spanish-Spanish, and that makes a difference. And even among native Spanish painters, González is exceptional. Most of them live and work in Spain; he has chosen to live and work in, of all places, Edinburgh. Not that there is anything wrong with Edinburgh as a place to live and work: quite the contrary. But there does seem, at least in terms of stereotypes, to be an odd irony in the fact that, while so many Northern artists dream of the warm South and the flooding Mediterranean light, what González appreciates is the clear, cold light of Scotland, the light that endistances and defines rather than smoothing away rough edges and dissolving form into colour.

Of course, we should not let national stereotypes run away with us. Not all Spaniards are passionate, excitable, sun-loving: remember the Inquisition, the stifling rituals of the Spanish court, the dark sides of Spanish art, from Zurbarán to Goya. In certain respects González is closer to this old tradition of aristocratic restraint than to the passionate prodigality of Picasso. And thus, curiously distant from the preoccupations and priorities of Spanish artists in general during the explosion of activity which has followed the death of Franco. By an odd trick of circumstance, the art Establishment in Franco's last years had become, not, as one might expect, bombastic naturalists celebrating the glories of blood and state along lines approved in Nazi Germany and Communist Russia, but rather the lyrical abstractionists of the school of Cuenca. (Pretty patterns with no political content were at least, presumably, safe.) So the young rebels of later generations were vowed, one way or another, to representation, usually, if belatedly, in a vaguely Pop Art or Neo-Expressionist style. And some of them, as you might expect, have used the new freedoms to express in paint the fact that they are gay.

ROBERTO GONZÁLEZ FERNÁNDEZ

La mayoría de los artistas hispánicos que mejor conocemos y vemos más — Botero, Claudio Bravo — son en realidad latino americanos. Roberto González Fernández es español de España y ahí está la diferencia. Incluso entre los mismos pintores españoles, González es una excepcíon. La mayoría viven y trabajan en España. El, del mundo entero, ha elegido Edimburgo. No es que sea una equivocación elegir esta ciudad como lugar de residencia y trabajo, quizás todo lo contrario. Pero parece, por lo menos a nivel general, una extraña ironía, el hecho de que mientras muchos artistas del Norte, sueñan con el caluroso Sur y la envolvente luz del Mediterraneo, lo que González aprecia es la clara y fría luz de Escocia: la luz que distancia y define en vez de desvanecer los perfiles y disolver les formas en color.

Naturalmente no tenemos que dejarnos influenciar por estereotipos nacionales. No todos los pintores españoles, siguen la vertiente oscura del arte hispano desde Zurbarán a Goya. Sin embargo en algunos aspectos, González se encuentra más cerca de esta vieja tradición de restricción aristocrática, que de la exuberancia apasionada de un Picasso. Y con ello está curiosamente alejado de las preocupaciones y prioridades de los artistas españoles en general, durante le explosión de actividad que aparece tras la muerte de Franco. Por una serie de casualidades y coincidencias, 'el arte oficial' durante los últimos años del régimen de Franco, estaba muy lejos de lo que cabría esperar: un bombardeo de realismo socialista celebrando las glorias del estado y de la raza, siguiendo las lineas de una Alemania nazi o de una Rusia comunista. En cambio, imperaba una linea de abstracción lírica, desarrollada alrededor de la Escuela de Cuenca, (placenteras formas decorativas sin contenido político, no resultaban ser comprometedoras). Tal vez por ello, los rebeldes de las generaciones siguientes se han comprometido de una u otra manera con la figuración, normalmente, aunque de manera soslayada, dentro

González, to this extent, might seem to fit in well with the current art scene in Spain. He is undoubtedly a representational painter. He is also unmistakably a gay painter: the very first works of his shown in a major London gallery were in fact images from a Gay Day parade in Los Angeles. But his approach would be noticeably out of pace in a country where the noisiest assertion of gay identity in art comes from the couple calling themselves Costus, who exemplify their own art movement, Chochonismo (literally ''cuntism'') by painting tourist images of saints and flamenco dancers on velvet and doing all sorts of other rather datedly camp things. In such a context González's attitude seems one of incredible cosmopolitan sophistication.

His art may be gay; it is very definitely not camp. And the gay elements are clearly subsumed into the aesthetic. Certainly at one level he is portraying, frequently nude, a lot of very attractive young men. But the homo-eroticism implicit in the subject-matter never slops over into a lazy, quasi-pornographic kind of painting, where the artist relies on merely pushing the usual buttons to get the usual automatic responses from an audience already sympathetic and just asking to be stimulated. In fact, González is a thoroughly classical artist, referring back to the great tradition of academic draughtsmanship as it would have been understood by Ingres or Flandrin. And consequently, though we would reasonably assume in this self-conscious age that someone portraying such subject-matter in such a way must necessarily be gay, historically that is not necessarily so.

Many visitors to the recent major show of the nineteenth-century academic Bouguereau in Paris or North America were excited to speculation: surely, to have drawn nude men with such loving care and detail he must have been…? Many more have wondered about the, as far as we can tell, unimpeachably heterosexual Brangwyn, who certainly loved to draw muscular torsoes and the like. But the point is, not necessarily. The artist's turn-on is often far different from the man's, even if artist and man happen to be the same person. And so, though obviously González's work does have a special appeal to gay spectators, that is not the perimeter of its appeal: the anecdote has been transcended, and what remains unarguable is the art.

In more contemporary terms, the comparisons which immediately present themselves are with the international school of Super-realists: even in Spain we find artists like Antonio López García, whose exquisitely precise

de un estilo neoexpresionista o cercano al Pop Art. Y algunos de ellos, como bien se podría anticipar, han utilizado sus recientemente adquiridas libertades para expresar en pintura sus preferencias sexuales.

González, desde este punto de vista, está integrado dentro del panorama español de las artes plásticas. Es, indudablemente, un pintor figurativo y en su obra se refleja una sensibilidad gai. Ya en su primera exposición en una importante galería de Londres, mostraba unas imágenes inspiradas en la 'Gay Day Parade' de Los Angeles. Sin embargo, su mundo de intereses no parecía estar en consonancia con lo que ocurría en su país a este respecto. Allí triunfaba el folclorismo y la exuberancia del Chochonismo de los Costus, pintando turísticas imágenes de santos y bailarinas flamencas, todo ello montado alrededor de un trasnochado espectáculo de locas. En este contexto la actitud de González resulta de un increíble cosmopolitismo.

En su obra puede haber elementos gais pero no hay definitivamente ningún rasgo folclórico. Y estos elementos estan perfectamente integrados en la estética de su pintura. Ciertamente nos muestra a veces hombres desnudos, pero el homoeroticismo implícito en la temática nunca cae en una pintura pseudopornográfica donde el artista hace uso de una serie de tópicos, para conseguir las respuestas automáticas de un público ganado de antemano, que solo espera ese estímulo. En realidad González es un profundo artista clásico, que conecta con la gran tradición del dibujo académico. Aunque se podría asumir con facilidad en estos tiempos de autoconocimiento, que cualquier artista que se interese por estos temas tiene que ser gai, historicamente esto no ha sido necesariamente la regla.

Muchos visitantes de la gran exposición dedicada al pintor académico del siglo XIX Bouguereau, tanto en Paris como en Estados Unidos, se han debido preguntar con curiosidad si su gran interés por el desnudo masculino podría significar una determinada preferencia sexual. Otros ya lo habian hecho con Brangwyn que ciertamente disfrutaba pintado espectaculares torsos masculinos, y del que nadie pone en duda sus tendencias heterosexuales. La cuestión es que no habría que relacionar una cosa con otra. Los intereses del hombre y artista no tienen porque coincidir aunque sean la misma persona. Por ello aunque obviamente la obra de González puede gustar a un espectador gai, su atractivo alcanza otros niveles: la anecdota ha sido trascendida y lo que permanece es, sin lugar a duda, su arte.

draughtsmanship is applied mostly to landscapes, interiors and still-lifes. But the comparison holds good only on a purely technical level: González's fundamental vision is quite different. Often it seems that he is a Surrealist rather than a Super-realist: the observation has become so close that we come out the other side of realism, on the dark side of the moon. There may well be nothing you can precisely put your finger on. The series of blue/grey-toned pictures of young men, usually alone though maybe about to encounter, among the chill classical towers and colonnades of Edinburgh, for instance, have nothing absolutely unreal about them. And yet there is an irreducible strangeness which is never possible entirely to explain away. And the men in rooms, dressed or undressed, alone or in ambiguous groups, do not seem quite to belong to the world we live in.

Part of the elusive atmosphere which pervades González's recent works may well derive from his literary inspirations, in the Bible or in the writings of poets such as Cavafy or Cernuda. But the intricate titles of his later paintings seem to be applied after the germination of the image, to signal some correspondence of thought or feeling, rather than that the picture is to be regarded as in any way an illustration of the text. And this is quite right and proper. As González says, he is in many respects an autobiographical painter, though the autobiography in question is evidently a spiritual and emotional progression rather than a catalogue of external events. However much, in his physical person, he may go out and about in the company of men, his mind seems to be a twilight zone, less tormented, perhaps, but no less dark and mysterious than of, say, Edvard Munch. It is González's singular skill, and our singular blessing, that he has been about to bring it out into the chill light of Edinburgh, and put it down on canvas with such discipline, precision and grace. No sloppy, superficial emotion here, but who can doubt that the banked fires of passion are smouldering underneath.

John Russell Taylor

En términos más actuales, si hubiera que encontrar una escuela en la que encuadrarlo, podria hacerse a primera vista, entre los hiperrealistas. Incluso en España encontramos a un Antonio López García cuya exquisita y precisa utilización del dibujo está puesta principalmente al servicio del paisaje, del bodegón y de la escena de interior. Pero este paralelismo solo se mantiene a un nivel puramente técnico. La idea que respalda la obra de González es fundamentalmente distinta. A menudo parece estar más cerca del surrealismo que del hiperrealismo; su observación es tan profunda que nos lleva al otro lado del realismo, a la cara oculta de la Luna. Y sin embargo, no hay nada específico que lo delate. En su serie en tonos azul grisaceos. por ejemplo, nos muestra a jóvenes, a menudo solos, quizás a punto de encontrarse con alguien entre las frias torres y columnatas clásicas de Edimburgo, sin que se pueda hallar nada absolutamente irreal en ellos. Sin embargo nos trasmiten una sensación de extrañeza dificil de explicar. Y los hombres, en habitaciones, vestidos o desnudos, solos o no, no parece que pertenezcan totalmente, al mundo en que vivimos.

Puede que esta atmósfera inquietante que se respira en los últimos trabajos de González esté provocada en parte por sus inspiraciones literarias: En la Biblia primero y más tarde a través de la poesía de escritores como Cernuda o Cavafy. Pero los complejos títulos de sus obras parecen haber sido elegidos después de la germinación de la imágen, señalando una correspondencia de pensamiento o un sentimiento común, por lo que no se puede de ninguna manera ver la imágen como una ilustración de ese texto. Y esto es lo adecuado y correcto. Como el mismo González opina, él es, en muchos aspectos, un pintor autobiográfico, aunque esa característica es sólo evidente como una progresión espiritual y emocional, más que como un catálogo de hechos específicos. Si a nivel personal sobresale una apariencia de tranquilidad, rodeado de amigos, su mente, sumergida en una zona de penumbra, nos lleva en cambio, a un mundo, menos atormentado que, por ejemplo, un Munch, pero no por ello menos obscuro y misterioso. Hemos tenido la suerte de que gracias a su habilidad, ese mundo haya podido salir a la fria luz de Edimburgo, trasladándolo al lienzo con enorme disciplina, precisión y sabiduría. Aquí no hay emociones superficiales, pero quién puede dudar que contenidas pasiones se funden en su interior.

John Russell Taylor

ROBERTO GONZÁLEZ FERNÁNDEZ IN CONVERSATION WITH JAVIER MAZORRA

JM Your works appear to be more and more timeless emblems — frozen yet passional. In another way they are works that could only have been created in the last quarter of this century. How aware are you of this?

RGF I'm interested in creating images with the strength and coherence that make them stand on their own, open to different interpretations. I omit all unnecessary elements, reducing them to a minimum and, maybe, creating a timeless emblematic character. However this must be seen in the historic and geographic framework of my particular time and place. Painting is my form of expression and my works show all that I care for, like and am concerned with at a personal level.

JM Since the beginning of the seventies and after a brief expressionistic period, you have been working, apparently, in the same style and on the same subjects. How do you see your career and what about this continuity?

RGF When I was at art school I thought I had found in the expressionistic manner the style suitable for the work I wanted to do. I worked in this style for about two years though it didn't take long for me to realize its limitations. At the same time at the art school (Madrid), a group of artists were working against the stream, in a realistic style which opened up a new field of possibilities for me. I searched for an ideal medium and technique for my work until I found the one I use at present. This consists of a base of inks and pencils on paper. Despite having worked in oil for some time, I am not interested in the quality it offers me, I try precisely to get away from its painterly textures.

JAVIER MAZORRA EN CONVERSACION CON ROBERTO GONZÁLEZ FERNÁNDEZ

JM Da la impresión de que tus obras son, cada vez más, emblemas intemporales en donde congelas el tiempo, manteniendo el elemento pasional. Por otro lado, son obras que no podrían haber sido creadas mas que por alguien en el último cuarto del siglo veinte. ¿ Hasta que punto eres consciente de todo esto?

RGF En primer lugar lo que me interesa crear son imágenes, con la fuerza y la coherencia que las haga autosuficientes, abiertas a múltiples interpretaciones. Elimino todo lo superfluo, limitando los elementos de composición al mínimo, creando quizás, ese caracter emblemático e intemporal. De todas maneras está visto dentro del momento histórico y geográfico en el que vivo y eso tiene que quedar reflejado.
   Por otro lado, pintar es mi manera de expresión y en mi obra queda plasmado todo lo que me interesa, me gusta y me preocupa, a un nivel claramente personal.

JM Desde principios de los setenta y tras un breve período expresionista, estás trabajando, aparentemente, dentro de una misma línea tanto formal como temática. ¿ Cómo ves tu trayectoria y hasta que punto es cierta esa linealidad?

RGF En un primer momento de aprendizaje, de todos los estilos que se me ofrecían, el que más me atrajo fué el expresionismo, en el cual trabajé durante un par de años, aunque no tardé en ver sus limitaciones para lo que quería expresar. Al mismo tiempo había en la escuela de BB.AA. de Madrid, un grupo de artistas, que contra toda corriente, trabajaban dentro de una linea realista, que me abrió un nuevo campo lleno de posibilidades. Desde entonces he ido buscando el medio y la técnica más idónea para realizar mi obra, hasta encontrar la que utilizo actualmente, a base de tintas y lápices, con la que me encuentro perfectamente identificado. Por el momento, la plasticidad que me ofrece el óleo no me interesa, precisamente intento apartarme de su calidad pictorica.

Untitled   1973
pencil   (43 x 32)cm

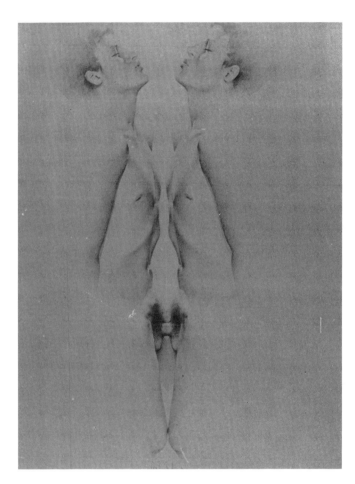

Calle Canal   1974
Canal Street
pencil   (58 x 35)cm

JM Nevertheless, in your recent work, despite the use of your mixed technique, there is an unmistakable painterly quality, maybe due to a wider range of colours or the mixture of brush work and strokes more open and spontaneous. How do explain this apparent contradiction?

RGF I think there is coherence in my work at both a formal and conceptual level, but there is also a continuous evolution. The use of a richer range of colour is the answer to certain needs that arise without distorting the basic image which is still close to reality.

JM It is not difficult to make out a different series of pictures clearly defined without having to consider their technical aspect. Is there any reason for it?

RGF Yes, as my work is the reflection of my life and with the perspective given by time, I can see that each one of these series belong to very specific moments, related to external clues; a first trip to the USA in 1972 introduced me to pop images such as base ball players and all American boys that are the base for three series in black & white. Later I quit my onlooker role to become a participant.
     First in a world with two faces divided by facades, walls, windows with reflections of that double personality. Afterwards moonlight appears and the slightly sordid night scene, blind alleys where the only hope comes from the sky above. My military service in North Africa also started a new series and forced situations to happen in even closer surroundings, more oppressed still.
     And, in 1977 a complete change in my life: I move to Edinburgh; change my technique, return to oil painting and lose myself in all kinds of mazes...

JM Yes, it seems that during that time, in your work man is subjected to the architectural frame that surrounds him. Even if man goes sporadically out of stage he is usually the protagonist of your images, is he not?

RGF Yes, but more than man himself - you see what I am really interested in are human relationships. Since I am more involved with men, unfailingly, these have to come up in my work as reflections of my life. Nevertheless there are exceptions.

JM This must be the reason why your image comes up so often in your pictures. Are they related to specific situations or is it something more elaborate?

RGF The start of each picture is usually a life experience or an idea, that I try to transform in a situation that goes above the anecdote, getting a new dimension and who better than myself to represent my own experiences. Though I believe that the least important thing is who appears, what matters is the concept backing the image.

JM En tus últimas obras sin embargo, a pesar de la utilización de tu tecnica mixta hay un innegable elemento pictórico, ya sea por la aparición de la gama de colores más amplia o por la mezcla de calidades y trazos, cada vez más abiertos y libres. ¿ Como explicas esta contradicción?

RGF Creo que en mi obra hay una total coherencia tanto a nivel técnico como temático, pero también una continua evolución. La mayor utilización del color, responde a una serie de necesidades que aparecen, sin desvirtuar la imagen que sigue sujeta a una realidad.

JM Volviendo a tu trayectoria, aparte de la evolución técnica, no es dificil agrupar tu obra en períodos bastante concretos. ¿ Esto a que responde?

RGF Mi obra es el reflejo de mi vida y con la perspectiva que da el tiempo, puedo ver que cada uno de estos grupos pertenece a momentos muy determinados, que responden a claves exteriores: un primer viaje a Estados Unidos en 1972 me introduce a unas imágenes tan populares como los beisbolistas y 'All American boys' que son la base para tres series en blanco y negro. Más tarde dejo de ser espectador y paso a ser participante. Primero en un mundo con dos caras, dividido por fachadas, muros, ventanas como soporte de reflejos de esa doble personalidad.
     Después aparece la luz de luna y los ambientes un tanto sórdidos de la noche, patios en donde la única esperanza de libertad viene desde el cielo. El servicio militar en el norte de Africa, abre un nuevo período y obliga a que las situaciones se desarrollen en ambientes totalmente cerrados, aun mas oprimidos. Y en 1977, cambio total de vida, me voy a vivir a Edimburgo, cambio total de técnica, vuelvo al óleo perdiendome en todo tipo de laberintos . . .

JM Si, parece que durante ese tiempo el hombre esta supeditado al marco arquitectónico que le rodea. Aunque esporadicamente desaparece, el hombre es casi siempre el protagonista exclusivo de tus imágenes. ¿ A que se debe esa realidad?

RGF Bueno, más que el hombre, lo que me interesa son las relaciones humanas. Desde el momento en que mi mayor relación es con hombres, estos indefectiblemente tienen que aparecer en mi obra como reflejo de mi vida, aunque por supuesto hay excepciones.

JM Si, eso debe explicar tu continua aparición en tus cuadros. ¿ Son reflejo de situaciones específicas o es algo más complejo?

RGF El punto de partida de cada cuadro suele ser una vivencia o idea concreta que intento transformar en una situación que, por encima de la mera anécdota, adquiera una nueva dimensión. Y ¿ quién mejor que yo para representar mis propias vivencias? Aunque creo que lo menos importante es quién aparezca, lo que cuenta es el concepto que respalda la imagen.

En mis noches secretamente encontradas   1975
In my secretly founded nights
pencil and ink   (50 x 70)cm

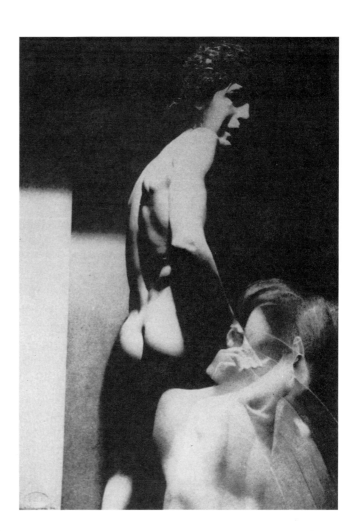

Tovar VII   1976
pencil and ink   (50 x 35)cm

JM Then, can we consider that there is a primacy of concept beyond the image itself?

RGF I don't think we can separate one thing from the other. And although the idea behind a picture is very important, the creative process containing it is equally essential.

I take great care in the formal, nearly theatrical composition of each picture. It is not difficult to discover some of my obsessions — like number three, or in diagonal, or lines of vision that go beyond the picture...and the quite unusual use of colour with a non realistic character, more like an emotional element.

JM Between 1979 and 1981 you made two series that are very different to what you have done earlier on: *Elephant Walk* and *Parade*. How did this happen?

RGF After I left the maze I was in, a summer in California opened the gates to a new way of life. What I saw is shown more symbolically in the pictures of Castro houses in San Fransisco and more directly in *Parade*. Despite being an homage to everything I found there and specifically the sexual-political awareness which at that time was at its peak, I also wanted to state its frailty, its external superficiality. It was a very special time, very enjoyable, essential for the gay subculture but with the ephemeral connotations that are attached to every parade.

JM Since then it is quite clear that you get the stability that allows you to retake the path that had been temporarily closed since you moved to Edinburgh.

RGF Yes, man is back in his entirety, undisputed, on his own, nothing to do with the parade scene where he appeared intermingled or confused with the surrounding architecture. At the beginning using the Bible as a base, I displayed a number of situations taking into account man's need for communication, going deep into relationships of dependency.
Since then I work more specifically on the idea of man as a friend and comrade(companion). A theme that for the time being is far from being exhausted and where I still see an endless number of possibilities.

JM ¿ Se puede considerar entonces que tiene preeminencia el concepto sobre la imagen en tu obra?

RGF Realmente creo que no puede separarse una cosa de la otra. Y aunque el concepto es muy importante tambien lo es el proceso creativo que lo contiene. Insisto mucho en la composición formal, casi escenográfica de cada cuadro. No es dificil descubrir pequeñas obsesiones que aparecen constantemente, como el número tres, composiciones en triángulo o en diagonal, lineas de visión fuera del cuadro . . . y la particular utilización del color con caracter no realista, sino como un elemento emocional . . .

JM Entre 1979 y 1981 aparecen dos series muy diferentes a todo lo que habías hecho anteriormente: *Elephant Walk* y *Parade*. ¿ A que se debe?

RGF Trás el laberinto en el que estaba metido, es un verano en California lo que me abre las puertas a otra manera de vida. Lo que veo lo reflejaré, de una manera mas simbólica en las casas de Castro de San Fransisco y más directamente en *Parade*. Sin dejar de ser un homenaje a todo lo que encuentro allí y en especial al movimiento de política sexual que alcanzaba su punto álgido en aquel momento; quería dejar patente la fragilidad y temporalidad a que este estaba sometido. Fué un momento muy concreto, muy importante para la subcultura gai pero con las connotaciones efímeras de todo desfile.

JM Desde entonces queda bastante claro que alcanzas la estabilidad que te permite retomar el camino que había quedado temporalmente cerrado desde tu llegada a Edimburgo.

RGF Si, el hombre vuelve a aparecer en su plenitud, indivualizado, nada que ver con las escenas de Parade en donde se mezcla y confunde en exteriores. En un principio utilizando como base la Biblia, desarrollo una serie de situaciones partiendo de la necesidad de comunicación del hombre, ahondando en sus relaciones de dependencia.
Desde entonces trabajo más concretamente en la idea del hombre como amigo y compañero, un tema que por el momento no solo no he agotado, sino en el que aún veo infinitas posibilidades.

Come shoot your works off, house   1979
pencil   (38.3 x 23)cm

It's Hot   1979
pencil   (38 x 28)cm

Esa semana dure todavía   1977
That week's still on
pencil and ink   (94 x 71)cm

Untitled   1976
pencil and ink   (50 x 70)cm

Untitled   1976
pencil and ink   (50 x 69)cm

Untitled   1976
pencil and ink   (50 x 35)cm

Vuelvo a ser el que siempre he querido ser   1977
I'm again the one I always wanted to be
oil   (76 x 97)cm

Come shoot your works off   1980
(First meeting in Mme Du Barry's bedroom)
oil   (56 x 73)cm

Parade X   1981
pencil and crayon   (74 x 53)cm

20

A rainbow of sexual preferences II   1980
Un arco iris de preferencias sexuales II
pencil and ink   (53 x 38)cm

David and Saul   1981
And David came to Saul, and he stood before him:
And he loved him greatly
David y Saúl
pencil and ink   (75 x 53)cm

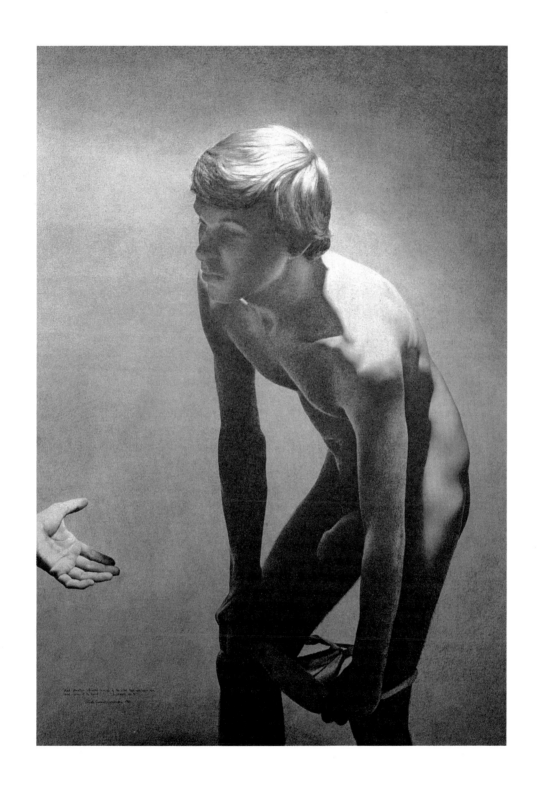

David and Jonathan III   1981
And Jonathan stripped himself of the robe that was upon him, and
he gave it to David (I Samuel 18,2)
David y Jonatán III
pencil and ink   (75 x 53)cm

David and Jonathan I   1981
That the soul of Jonathan was knit with the soul of David, and
Jonathan loved him as his own soul (I Samuel 18,1)
David y Jonatán I
pencil and ink   (25 x 35)cm

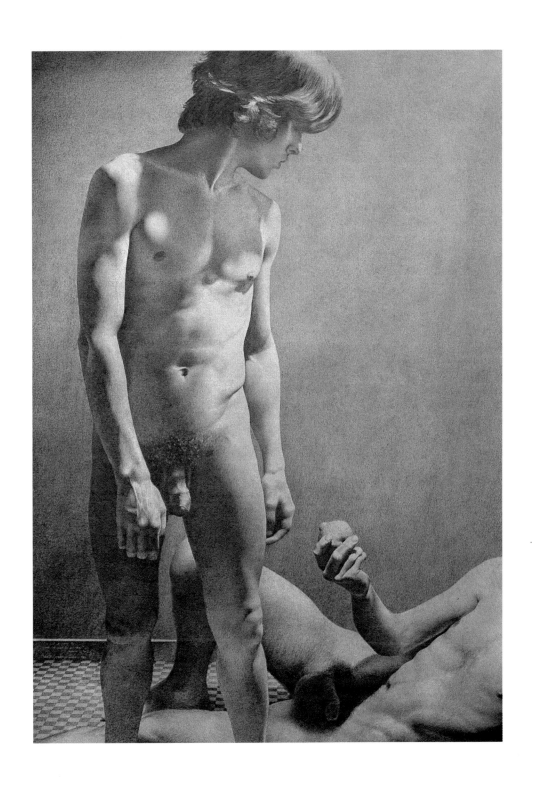

The original sin   1981
Ye shall not surely die . . . And ye shall be as Gods (Gen 3,4-5)
El pecado original
pencil and ink   (75 x 53)cm

Lazarus resurrection   1981
And he that was dead came forth, bound hand and foot with
graveclothes: and his face was bound about with a napkin
(St John 11,44)
Resurección de Lázaro
pencil and ink   (75 x 53)cm

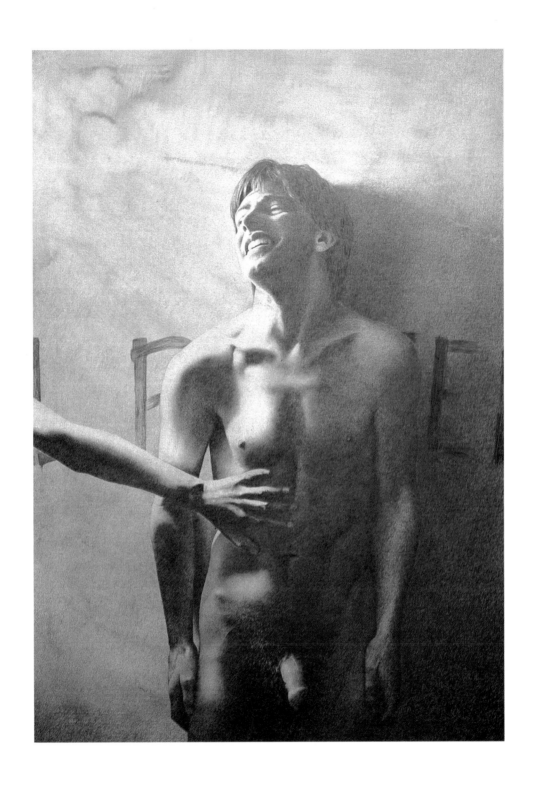

Adam's discovery of pleasure   1981
. . . And man became a living soul (Gen 2,7)
Creación de Adám
pencil and ink   (75 x 53)cm

27

Alla, alla lejos donde habite el olvido   1982
There, far away where oblivion lives
pencil and ink   (106 x 150)cm

Trangando sueño tras un vidrio impalpable/Entre las dobles fauces/
Tuyas, pereza, de ti también, costumbre   1982
Swallowing dreams behind an untouchable glass/Between the
double mouths/Yours, laziness, of you also a habit
pencil and ink   (85 x 173)cm

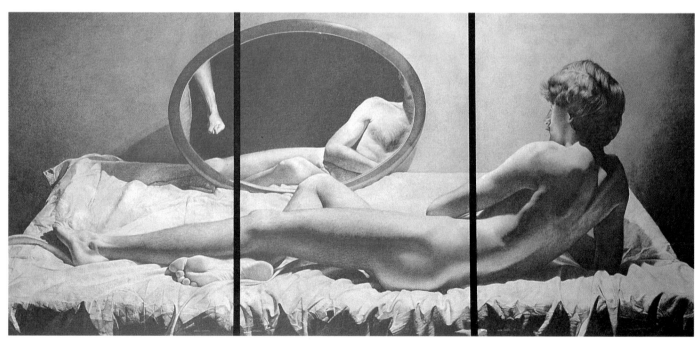

Otros cuerpos, corsario, nada saben (I & II)   1982
Other bodies, corsair, know nothing about it
pencil and ink   (74 x 162)cm

Mitad y mitad/Sueño y sueño/Carne y carne   1982
Half and half/Dream and dream/Flesh and flesh
pencil and ink   (85 x 173)cm

Placeres prohibidos/Planetas terrenales/Miembros
de marmol con sabor de estio   1982
Forbidden pleasures/earthly planets/marmoreal members with a taste of summer
pencil and ink   (85 x 175)cm

Figuras esculpidas   1982
Sculptured figures
pencil and ink   (75 x 53)cm

Viértete, viértete sobre mis deseos   1983
Flow, flow on my desires
pencil and ink   (160 x 75)cm

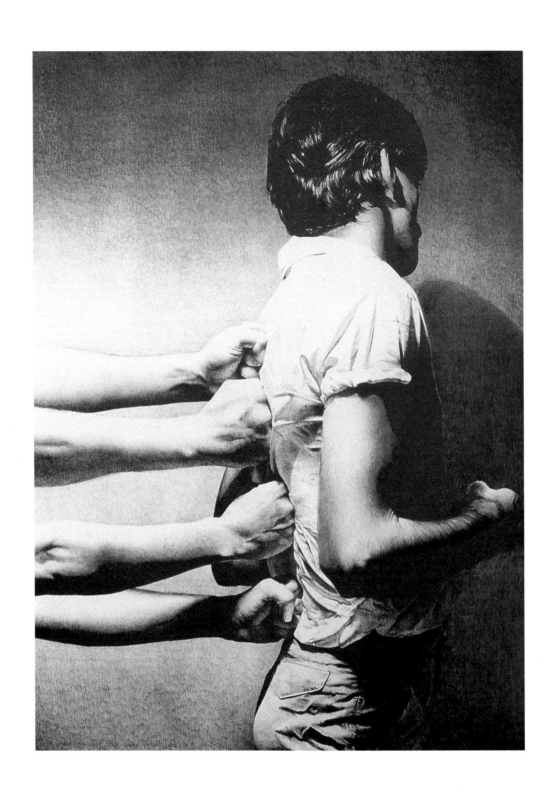

Una mano dará el poder de la sonrisa   1983
A hand will give the power of the smile
lithograph   (76.5 x 57)cm

No sabía los límites impuestos   1983
He didn't know the imposed limits
lithograph   (76.5 x 57)cm

Me sentirás   1983
You will feel me
lithograph   (76.5 x 57)cm

36

Mas hielo para sus corazones   1983
More ice for their hearts
pencil and ink   (107 x 75)cm

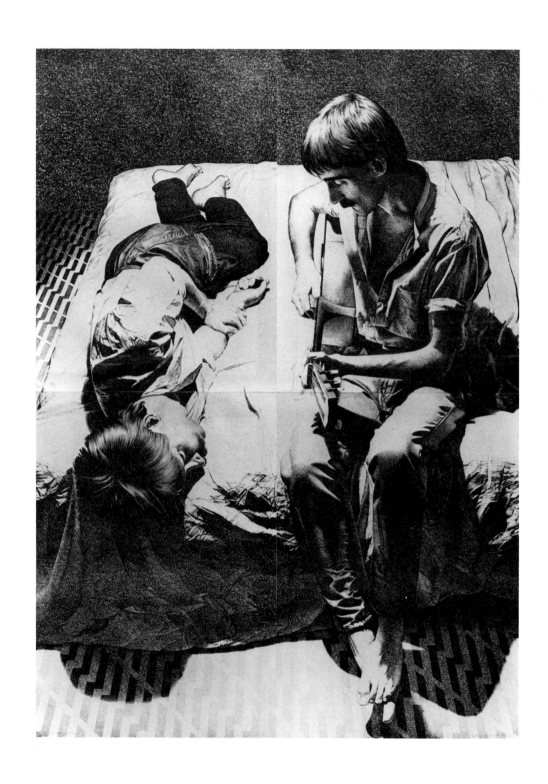

Otro vacío estrechan   1984
Tightening another emptiness
lithograph   (152 x 114)cm

El don de la palabra   1985
Between your youth and my desires
pencil and ink   (107 x 75)cm

Formando un solo ser de dos impulsos   1984
Making a single being from two beats
pencil and ink   (75 x 160)cm

Su perceptible paso por un cuerpo   1985
His perceivable print in a body
pencil and ink   (106 x 150)cm

No verás nada parecido en tu camino   1985
You will not see anything like it in your way
pencil and ink   (75 x 53)cm

No fueron obeliscos   1985
They were not obelisks
pencil and ink   (109 x 75)cm

Había pedido la tregua de la noche   1986
He had requested the truce of the night
pencil and ink   (109 x 75)cm

Se introdujo en la anémona   1986
He got into the anemone
pencil and ink   (109 x 75)cm

Y la ciudad al fondo inacabable   1986
And the city in the background unfinishable
pencil and ink   (109 x 74)cm

Soy los que nunca he sido   1986
I am the ones I have never been
pencil and ink   (75 x 53)cm

Reposa y sueña, un bosque una fuente   1986
Rest and dream, a wood a spring
pencil and ink   (109 x 75)cm

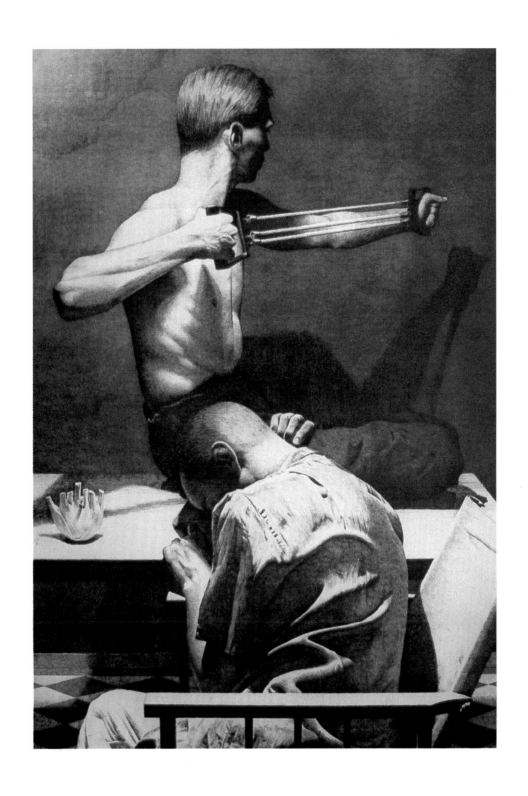

Let him gaze his fill   1986
etching   (98 x 68)cm

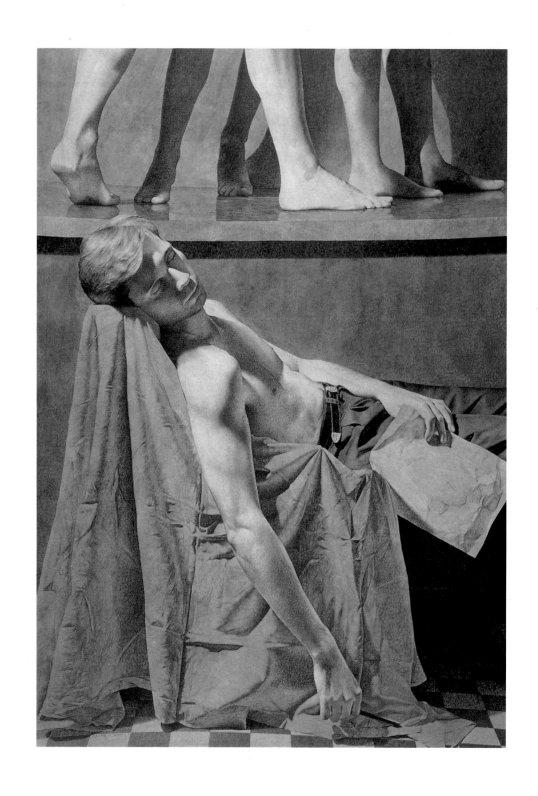

Homenaje a David   1987
Homage to David
pencil and ink   (109 x 75)cm

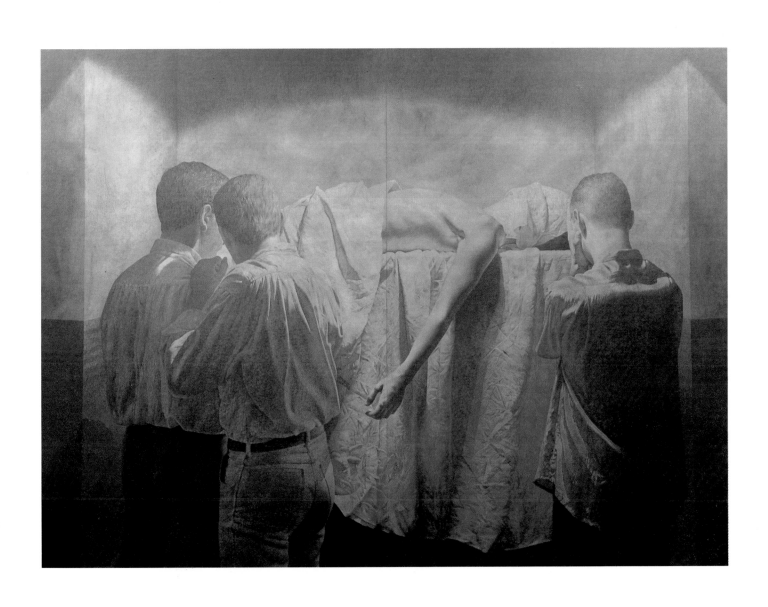

En la costa del Helesponto   1986 - 87
On the shore of the Hellespont
pencil and ink   (109 x 150)cm

Ha comenzado la del abismo   1987
Chaos has started
pencil and ink   (75 x 53)cm

Este condena de silencio   1987
This sentence of silence
pencil and ink   (109 x 75)cm

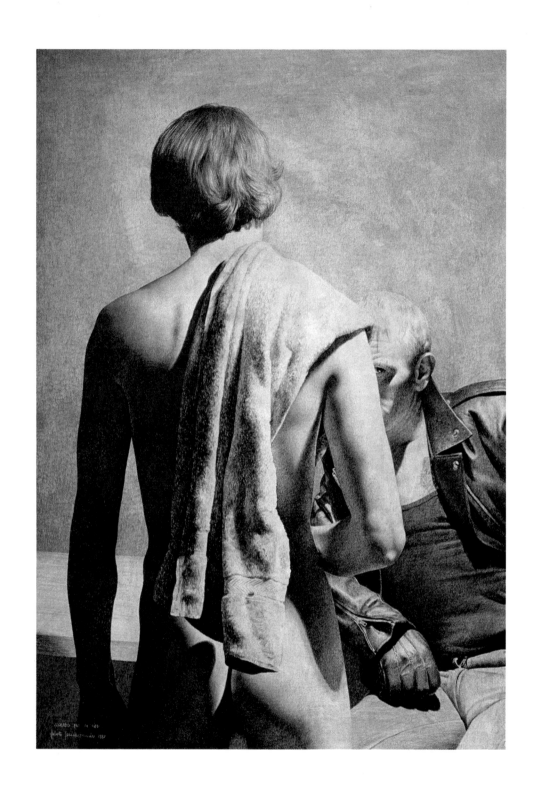

Asolado qué el ojo   1987
Ravaged was the eye
pencil and ink   (75 x 53)cm

THE ARTIST

photo of the artist by Carlos Diez Bustos

1948   born, Monforte de Lemos (Spain)
1969-74   studied Fine Arts at Escuela Superior de Bellas Artes de San Fernando, Madrid
1977   moved to Edinburgh.
1982   lives and works in Madrid and Edinburgh
1984   awarded grant by New York Foundation for the Arts

At present works with Nicholas Treadwell Gallery in Great Britain and with Galería Leandro Navarro in Spain.

One person shows

1967   Galería Artes, La Coruña.
1975   La Casa del Siglo XV, Segovia
1987   Galería Egam, Madrid
          Galería Simancas, Santander
1980   Henderson Gallery, Edinburgh
1981   Gallery 20, Brighton
          Henderson Gallery, Edinburgh
          Rob Gallery, Amsterdam
1982   Henderson Gallery, Edinburgh
1983   Galerie Etienne de Causans, Paris
1984   ARCO 84, Galería Esti-Arte, Madrid
          Galería Novecento, Vigo
          500 Gallery, Monmouth College, New Jersey
          Anderson Gallery, Bridgewater College, Massachusets
          Galería Novecento, Santiago
1985   Galería Quintero, Barranquilla (Colombia)
          Galería Caledonia, Bilbao
          The Printmakers Workshop, Edinburgh
          Galería Torculo, Madrid
1986   Glasgow Print Studio, Glasgow
1987   Botanique (Tels Quels), Brussells
          Galería Dieciseis, San Sebastian

Mixed exhibitions include:

1973   Galería Ausias March, Barcelona: 'Dibujos para nuestra decada I'
1975   Galería Barbié, Barcelona: 'Alrededor de la Realidad'
          Galerie Gilles Corbeil, Montreal: 'Jeunes Peintres Hyperréalistes Espagnols'
          Galería Ausia March, Barcelona: 'Dibujo II'
1976   'Realismo Español Contemporaneo'. Touring exhibition organised by the Spanish Ministry of Education & Science.
1978   La Casa del Siglo XV, Segovia: '15 años de la Casa del Siglo XV'.
1980   Henderson Gallery, Edinburgh: 'Erotic Art'
          Royal Scottish Academy, Edinburgh
          Fischer Fine Art, London: 'The Figurative Approach V'
          Edinburgh Arts Centre: 'Lothian Printmakers'
          Galerie Tendenz, Sindelfingen
1981   Scottish Arts Council: 'Edinburgh behind the Facade'
          Henderson Gallery, Edinburgh: 'Erotic Art II'
          Fischer Fine Art, London: 'Various Approaches'
          Nicholas Treadwell Gallery, London: 'The Artist as his own Model'
          Universidad Complutense, Madrid: 'Realismo en España'
1982   Angela Flowers Gallery, London: '80 Prints by Modern Masters'
          Galerie Etienne de Causans, Paris

1983   Nicholas Treadwell Gallery, London: 'Still Life — Still Art'
          City Art Gallery, New York: 'Britain Salutes New York'
          Scottish Arts Council: 'Grease and Water'
          Royal Academy, Edinburgh: 'Scottish Prints Now'
          Ebury Gallery, London: 'The Male Nude in Art'
          Nicholas Treadwell Gallery, London: 'Hallelujah and Amen'
1984   Galería Sur, Santander:
          Sala Pelaires, Palma de Mallorca: 'Figuraciones'
          Galería Moriarty, Madrid: 'Las Ciudades'
          Ateneo, Madrid: 'Cinco Grabadores'
1985   Spanish Foreign Affairs Ministry: 'Contemporary Spanish Graphics'
          Glasgow Print Studio: 'Glasgow'
          The Printmakers Workshop, Edinburgh: 'Points of View'
          Casa de la Cultura, Fuengirola: 'Tres Grabadores'
          Glasgow Print Studio: 'Unique & Original'
1986   Galería Dieciseis, San Sebastian: 'Cuatro Visiones de la Realidad'
          El Monte, Sevilla: 'IV Festival de la Pintura'
          Gallery of Modern Art, Rijeka: 'X International Drawing Exhibition'
          Glasgow Print Studio: 'The Clyde'
          Tuzla: '4 INTERBEP'
          Fundación Santillana e Centro Cultural de la Villa, Madrid: 'Voces Interiores. 12 Realistas Españoles'

International Art Fairs and Print Biennales

ARCO, Madrid — 1983, 84, 88.
ART BASLE — 1982, 83, 84, 85).
BATH ART FAIR — 1982, 83, 84, 85, 86
FIAC, Paris — 1982, 83, 84, 85, 86
INTERNATIONALER KUNSTMARK, Dusseldorf & Köln — 1982, 83, 84, 85, 86
LONDON ART FAIR — 1985, 86

Scottish Print Open — 1980, 83
Ljubljana Biennal of Graphic Art — 1981, 83, 85
Ibizagrafic — 1982, 84
International Print Exhibition, ROC Taipei — 1983, 85
Liége International Print Biennal — 1984
Fredrickstad Print Biennal — 1985
Cracow International Print Biennal — 1984, 86
Katowice Intergraphic — 1984, 86

Public Collections and Museums

Ely Art Gallery, Westfield State College, Mass., USA
Gallery of Modern Art, Skopje
Gallery of Modern Art, Ljubljana
Dundee City Art Gallery
Edinburgh City Arts Centre
Hunterian Art Gallery, Glasgow
Kelvingrove Art Gallery, Glasgow
Museo de BellasArtes de la Coruña
Gallery of Modern Art, Sevilla
Cabinete de Estampas de la Biblioteca Nacional, Madrid
Scottish Arts Council Collection
Fundación Lorenzana, Madrid
Denne Hill Collection, Kent(UK)
Forbes Collection, New York
Fife Regional Art Collection
Spanish Ministry of Foreign Affairs Collection
Fundación Colegio de Rey, Alcala de Henares
Cracow National Museum

INDEX TO ARTWORKS

PAINTINGS & DRAWINGS from

GMP — THE GAY MEN'S PRESS

Philip Core
PAINTINGS: 1975-1985
Introduced by George Melly
Philip Core is an ex-patriot American painter resident in London and his much-celebrated paintings are informed by strong gay cultural themes.
40 colour plates
(200 x 200)mm, 96 pages, £14.95 hardback

Mario Dubsky
TOM PILGRIM'S PROGRESS AMONG THE CONSEQUENCES OF CHRISTIANITY
Introduced by Edward Lucie-Smith
Mario Dubsky was struck down at the height of his artistic career by the deadly AIDS virus. This collection of his pencil drawings stands as a testament to his position as a powerful gay artist.
64 black & white plates
(240 x 225)mm, 84 pages, £4.95 paperback

Juan Davila
HYSTERICAL TEARS
Edited by Paul Taylor
Juan Davila is a gay Chilean artist now living and working in Australia. His paintings constantly knock the Western World's artistic establishment from a unique combination of third-world and gay consciousness. His work has won world-wide fame and notoriety and utterly shocked the Australian authorities.
35 colour plates
(200 x 200)mm, 108 pages, £7.95 paperback, £14.95 hardback

David Hutter
NUDES AND FLOWERS
Introduced by Edward Lucie-Smith
David Hutter is a master English watercolourist. This exquisite collection of delicate watercolours is primarily of the modern male nude combined with a series of tender flower paintings.
40 colour plates
(200 x 200)mm, 96 pages, £9.50 paperback

Michael Leonard
CHANGING
Introduced by Edward Lucie-Smith
These highly-charged pencil drawings of males undressing have won world-wide acclaim.
50 black & white plates
(200 x 200)mm, 112 pages, £7.95 paperback

Michael Leonard
PAINTINGS
The Artist in conversation with Edward Lucie-Smith
This is a comprehensive collection of Michael Leonard's paintings executed from the early 70s to the present day in the widely popular photo-realist style. Subject matter ranges from portraiture and townscapes to the male nude.
40 colour plates
(200 x 200)mm, 104 pages, £14.95 hardback

Cornelius McCarthy
INTERIORS
Introduced by Emmanuel Cooper
A modern painter whose work embodies exciting form, colour and content and informed throughout with a highly charged gay sensibility.
40 colour plates
(200 x 200)mm, 64 pages, £8.95 paperback, £14.95 hardback

Peter Samuelson
POST-WAR FRIENDS
Introduced by John Russell Taylor
These paintings and drawings capture something of the style, time and place of Britain in the two decades following World War II.
10 black & white / 20 colour plates
(210 x 148)mm, 48 pages £6.95

Douglas Simonson
HAWAII
Douglas Simonson's paintings and drawings focus on the Pacific male.
They are both visually stunning and quietly erotic and manage to bring to
the viewer something of the atmosphere of these beautiful Pacific islands
and their people.
40 colour plates
(200 x 200)mm, 64 pages, £8.95 paperback, £14.95 hardback.

Nick Stanley(ed)
OUT IN ART
Christopher Brown, Chris Corr, Norman, Richard Royle, Graham
Ward.
Five modern gay British artists. This widely acclaimed collection
embraces five very different visualities though all are embued with
contemporary gay consciousness and a vibrant homo-eroticism.
37 colour plates
(200 x 200)mm, 64 pages, £7.95 paperback, £14.95 hardback.

Emmanuel Cooper
THE LIFE & WORK OF
HENRY SCOTT TUKE
Henry Scott Tuke (1858 - 1929) was known in his time as 'the painter
of youth', and indeed this beautiful monograph by one of Britain's
leading gay art critics vindicates his reputation admirably. This is the
first ever collection of his famous paintings and most plates are in full
colour.
20 black & white / 36 colour plates
(256 x 228)mm, 72 pages, £18.95 hardback

PLEASE SEND FOR OUR COMPLETE CATALOGUE TO

GMP
P O BOX 247
LONDON N15 6RW

AND WE WILL FORWARD IT BY RETURN